CW00833619

CROSS-STEPPING YOUR WAY TO SUCCESS

THE POWER TO TRANSFORM YOUR LIFE ONE STEP AT A TIME!

CAROLYN BOWEN

Published 2021 by Reality Plus – A Next Chapter Imprint

Edited by Emily Fuggetta

Cover art by Cover Mint

To Tom, and My Family

Thank you for your love, support and encouragement.

This book is dedicated to an amazing woman, M.J. Evans, who has seen me through my darkest hours and brightest moments. Her love, kindness and generosity, and strength of faith have inspired me, my children, and countless others. I love her dearly and am honored to call her family.

INTRODUCTION

Cross-stepping is defined as a two-way street. It is a way of moving your weight forward and backward until you achieve success. This is typical knowledge for surfers of the longboard who succeed with this method to hang ten or other magnificent watersport feats.

The reference to cross-stepping in this book refers to the zigzag motions you'll master to become successful for who you are and were meant to become. Get ready to throw overboard anything that stands in your way of achieving your dreams of living a purposeful and successful life.

If you're reading this book, we've most likely traveled down similar roads and asked the question, *How do I start over again and become successful?* Or to phrase it differently, *How can I be successful at any age?*

Reinventing ourselves is not a one-time-and-you're-done process. We change with our personal relationships as they begin and end—age, health, business climate, and financial situation to say a few of our lifestyle choices. This is not a bad thing, depending on how we handle it.

For instance, how many times have you read or known people who've fought vigorously to get ahead, failed maybe more than once, yet finally reached their initial or perhaps revamped goals?

From presidents and athletes, to professionals in medicine, arts and entertainment, to biblical stories, age is not a deterrent to reinventing yourself at any age to enjoy a new lifestyle.

If you already intuitively know age doesn't clip your wings to soar to new heights and discover new horizons, feel free to skip the examples below and go to the next section – Chapter 1.

Success and age aren't mutually exclusive.

Consider the life of Abraham Lincoln. The self-educated Lincoln was an astute lawyer and politician and was later elected president of the United States.

Ronald Reagan became our then-oldest president, approaching his 70th birthday when he took office in 1981.

He had a long career as a politician, which followed his earlier career as an actor.

Vaclav Havel, after a distinguished career as a playwright, became president of Czechoslovakia at age 52, following the fall of the communist regime.

Scientist Alexander Fleming didn't make a breakthrough discovery until an advanced age, which seems to have been built on a lifetime of work and experience. Fleming discovered penicillin — the first antibiotic — by accident it was said. For his discovery, Fleming received the Nobel Prize in 1945, at age 64.

There is Jesus Borrego, who set the 1500-meter record for 45- to 50-year-old men when he was 46, in 2008. His time, 3:52:43, would have easily won him the gold medal for the event in the Summer Olympics of 1912, when the medal was awarded to 21-year-old Arnold Jackson for his time of 3:56:08.

Oscar Gomer Swahn, a Swedish shooter, competed in three Olympics and won six medals, including three gold ones. At age 72, he was not only the oldest medalist but the oldest Olympian ever.

The great dame of television Lucille Ball made her first dime as an actress when she reached forty years of age. Later she became the first millionaire actress in television when she negotiated the production rights to the "I Love Lucy" TV show as part of her salary package.

And no one can forget Colonel Harland David Sanders, founder of Kentucky Fried Chicken, now known as KFC. The Colonel founded the restaurant chain when he was 65 years of age and went on to become a multimillionaire.

Anna Mary Robertson Moses — better known as Grandma Moses — was a happy long-time embroiderer until arthritis made that painful and difficult. Instead of the needles, she took up the paint brush at the age of 75 in 1935. Untrained, but in the firm American tradition of primitive art, her paintings were discovered in a drugstore window a la Lana Turner by a prominent collector in 1938, and a New York gallery show led to worldwide fame. She continued painting until close to her death in 1961, at age 101. Although she started out selling her paintings for $2 or $3, depending on size, in 2006, one of her 3,600 paintings, "Sugaring Off" (1943), sold for $1.2 million.

Two other rags-to-riches stories from the arts include Bill Traylor, a former slave who started painting at age 83, and none other than Paul Cezanne, who would have been only a footnote in art history as a minor impressionist had he not lived long enough to produce his signature late-life still-life inspirations for the cubism of Picasso and Braque.

At age 80, former manicurist Clara Peller plied her trade for a commercial shot in a barbershop. The Dancer Fitzgerald ad agency noticed her feisty manners and remarkable voice and hired her as an actress. In 1984, at age 81, she made her iconic debut in a Wendy's commercial. Looking at a competitor's big bun with a small burger, she loudly asked, "Where's the beef?" Although her career was short when she died in 1987, Peller lived long enough to be in a few movies, make an appearance on WrestleMania, and get into a show-business controversy when she was dropped by Wendy's after making a commercial for Prego, saying she found the beef in their spaghetti sauce.

Wendy's founder Dave Thomas, another late bloomer in marketing at 57, appeared in more than 800 commercial advertisements for the chain from 1989 to 2002, more than any other company founder in television history. Thomas was previously affiliated with Colonel Sanders, for whom he designed the revolving chicken bucket before founding Wendy's at 37.

Novelist Harry Bernstein published a short story when he was only 24, in 1934. However, his well-received debut novel, *The Invisible Wall*, was published by Random House when he was 96 years old. The story was based on his childhood in England, before his family immigrated to the United States. Bernstein had kept his hand in as an editor and writer for trade publications. After his wife of 67 years died, a return to fiction and memories of his childhood was therapy for his loss and loneliness. He published three more books before his death at the age of 101. A fourth book "What Happened to Rose," was to be published posthumously in Italian by Edizioni Piemme in 2012, according to reports. In an interview with The New York Times, Bernstein said, "If I had not lived until I was 90, I would not have been able to write this book. It just could not have been done even when I was 10 years younger. I wasn't ready. God knows what other potentials lurk in other people, if we could only keep them alive well into their 90s."

And then there's Abraham and Sarah from the Holy Bible. The founder of the Jewish religion was living in Ur of the Chaldees when God spoke to the 75-year-old man then known as Abram and said, "Leave your country, your people and your father's household and go to the land I will show you. I will make you into a great nation and I will bless you." Abram moved with his barren wife Sarai, age 65, and a number of other relatives, including Lot, to Canaan, and the rest is biblical history. Losing all hope for providing Abraham an offspring, Sarai offered her servant Hagar to Abram, who gave birth to Ishmael, the father of Islam.

Sometime later after Ishmael's birth, Sarai at 90 years of age gave birth to Isaac, the promised son. Isaac's birth led to a new covenant with God including circumcision and name changes for the parents to Abraham and Sarah. Isaac went on to become the second patriarch of Judaism, followed by his son Jacob.

"The secret to a rich life is to have more beginnings than endings."
Dave Weinbaum

We've established there's potential for success at any age. The restructuring of our lives to fit our new vision of who we are now is a must. But how do we develop this vision and create the life we dream about?

Most of my adult life, I've been interested in what makes a person successful. Back in my college days, I wanted to research the cognitive processes of successful people (that is, what thoughts generated their success) but was influenced to look at another topic where research methods could be more easily applied.

That being said, I've experienced the pain of failure — more than once or twice. It's no big surprise that I'd want to know the answers that could lead to a successful life.

Nobody's perfect. How do I know this? I've tried living the perfect life, and it didn't work. Having held on to perfection stone-cold sober, while drinking, or dead drunk, it all turned out the same. I couldn't please everybody or live up to my own lofty expectations.

Who is a perfect person anyway, and by whose standards are you being defined? Are they yours or someone else's?

You first need to define what a successful life means to you individually. My definition is a life filled with peace, joy, good health, and financial freedom.

In this book you'll read about many of my findings, some from past educational pursuits and practical experience and others from mentors who appeared at the right moments in my life and made an impact.

"Whatever you are, be a good one."
Abraham Lincoln

1

HOW TO MASTER CROSS-STEPPING

Are you feeling like what you're doing just isn't working? If so, it's time to reinvent yourself. You can do this by following these suggestions for discovering your purpose — the person you were born to become.

I know you've heard the saying "life is short, make the most of today." As you grow older, this phrase becomes more meaningful, for you instinctively know that in some way it pertains to your happiness and success in life.

You'll want to get rid of outside influences that aren't relevant to your life goals. It's time to update your life and career plan. There is no age limit for creating a new you.

Remember to Make This Fun — You're Solving a Mystery!

5 Easy Steps

Step 1

My new definition of who I am as a person and new career options began with what I didn't want to do! For you, it may be just the opposite. However, this road map will get you to your destination.

Need prompting?

Using free-form writing, jot down the things you want to do and the things you don't want to do. They may or may not be related. For example: I know I want to be a well-read and beloved author and help others in their personal and professional growth. To learn what that meant for me, I began listing ideas for both plans. By identifying the things I wanted to do on one side and things I didn't want to do on the other, I began to see a pattern that provided a clear picture of my likes and dislikes.

For example, I know digital marketing is important for authors and businesses, but there are many companies fired up about offering this service. They stay on the cutting edge of marketing. The other part is that's not who I am. I don't have a passion for personally delivering the nuts and bolts, technical side of marketing. However, it's important for my business that I learn from these top marketers, and I do!

Another personal example for the "I like" column is helping others achieve their goals. Then I free-formed how I could do this. Perhaps, providing book reviews and tours for authors on my website and major social platforms would be helpful or sharing what I know about personal and professional development — like this book — would provide encouragement for others.

Step 2

Make a list of your present skills and training then cross-reference them to the ideas in your "I Like" column. Do you see an overlap between where you are now in lifestyle and career choices and future possibilities? If not, perhaps more research will answer your questions about earning the qualifications for doing what you want to do.

Ask what educational opportunities you need to accomplish the ideas from your "I Like" listing. Make adjustments by seeking the lessons/courses you need to make your career ideas a reality. If taking college courses isn't right for you, check out the numerous excellent eLearning courses, such as those offered through LinkedIn, or major experts in the area for which you need support. There are some good deals available for the cost-conscious professional. If cost is not a problem, there are freelancers and businesses you can hire to achieve results. However, remember knowledge is king, and you're protecting your business by knowing the "how-to" required to achieve the results you seek.

For example, as an author I need to know how to advertise, specifically on Amazon. I've taken the courses to get up and going but decided it was more technical and time-consuming than I desired. After all, this was taking me away from my writing life of putting words on paper. You guessed right, I hired a company to do it for me. This is one expense that's a must for me — the cost of doing business. As you can see, there are times you have to improvise to get the results you seek.

For marketing any product or service, I'd suggest creating a couple of campaigns yourself from what you've learned from researching the topic. Then compare the results with those of the company you hired to take over this aspect of marketing for you. If your outsourcer isn't doing better than the marketing campaigns you created, make changes, including finding a new marketing vendor.

As you go through the above process, your new plan will surface, and you'll find ways around obstacles.

Keep a journal of your thoughts and feelings. What ideas do you awaken with in the mornings? Jot those down, for the universe is trying to provide a roadmap for your next steps. The power of intention, according to the late Wayne Dyer, will lead you to the answers you seek.

. . .

Step 3

Make a list before you go to bed at night of what you'd like to accomplish the next day. Let your subconscious look for the answers as you sleep. Turn off any disturbances, like TV, radio, phone, etc. Let your mind rest. You'll thank me later! When I know you better (smiles), I'll share some true — but weird, you'll probably think — occurrences of this phenomenon using this concept.

Step 4

Arise early in the morning and journal your thoughts and feelings. Meditate — psychological studies show that taking the attitude of gratitude enhances your well-being. Give thanks for your new day and use this quiet time to reflect on your goals for the day. Breaking life patterns — including staying off the Internet during this time — was a huge change and challenge for me. I'd lost my way and had to get back to basics. Now I have more direction and focus for creating the lifestyle I want. You can too!

Step 5

Do some sort of physical exercises appropriate to your health level, such as stretching, cardio workouts, weight training, yoga or dance. Physical exercise has been shown to reduce depression and enhance focus. Plus, you'll love the way your body begins to look and your general feeling of well-being.

I hope these steps will guide you in reinventing yourself for the next phase of your life. Let me know your thoughts, hang-ups, and successes.

Sometimes you have to unfollow old dreams to pursue new ones!

2

LETTING GO OF THE PAST!

I KNOW THE FEELING OF WANTING TO SHUT OUT THE world and escape! I can tell you firsthand it can lead to depression, health problems and addictions.

Unfortunately, the ugly fact is you've got to deal with the hurts from the past. Just start with your earliest remembrance of successes and failures and go from there. As you do this, you'll most likely see a pattern and begin to read between the lines about what was motivating you toward success when all you received was failure.

Ask yourself, what's stopping you from living your dreams? Needing to let go of the past could be a culprit. I say this as one who never wanted to revisit my downfalls. That is until the day my entire world fell apart — the death of my closest loved one, business failure, family estrangements, being neck-deep in personal and business debt, and medical problems, including a stroke at an early age. (Yes, I had to learn to spell and type again, and my face was drooping on one side at the time.)

What's significant to me is I owe a small fortune for coursework completed for a Ph.D. to learn how to overcome problems and help others do the same. Yet, my help came from the Lord, who put a guardian angel (with a high-school education) in my life. I can't fall so far that she can't reach me with her wisdom and demanding attitude of "You can't quit now."

What I've Learned!

I've learned to stay humble and take bite-sized pieces to accomplish my goals. But to move forward I had to take a step back and clean house with the emotional and mental debris from the past.

I know you've heard this saying: you've got to put the past behind you before you can move on. How popular is that thought?

Google *put the past behind you*, and about 82 million results will pop up in less than a second. I think we all recognize this important concept yet are unwilling or unable to face it on our own. Sometimes, we receive prodding from the Universe to keep us from languishing in our turmoil. If we are lucky, friends, family, support groups, psychologists and others can help us clear the debris from the past so we can be fully present in our thoughts and feelings.

Letting go of the past is not a new concept. From Biblical times we are reminded that "...if we are faithful to Him and confess our sins, we will be forgiven and cleansed. Through prayer and spiritual growth, we can more easily put our past behind us and move forward to achieve the great things God has planned for us." (1 John 1:9)

In more recent history, Forrest Gump says this memorable line in his movie: "My mama always said you've got to put the past behind you before you can move on." Gump was referencing his run across America that took 3 years, 2 months, 14 days and 16 hours and covered 19,024 miles. While sitting on the bench waiting for the bus to reach Jenny's home, Gump tells his story of the run to others waiting, and he concludes, "I think that was what all that running was about."

His run was a way for him to put his past behind him. He instinctively understood that carrying the past was detrimental to his present and future.

So why is it so difficult to move on after defeat, heartbreak, or failures of any sort?

There are times we need help. I don't see this as a weakness but an understanding of our needs and desires to live a fulfilling life.

Sometimes we just need a starting place and a helping hand. Having failures of my own, I recognize the benefits of meditation, journaling, and someone you know who will be present for you.

There are some great books, especially the Bible, that'll inspire you when you're feeling low. Many of favorites are both spiritual and inspirational. For example, Joyce Meyer's "Living a Life You Love." Others are by leading motivational authors in personal and business motivation and finance.

Although it is difficult to look at our failures, we must examine the places we've missed the mark prior to planning our next venture and/or relationships. Thinking our problems stem from bad timing, people involved, place, money, etc., can be deceiving. Some or all of this may well be true, but do you want to carry this with you to your next relationship, career, business or family situation? I think not, for shadows from fragments of our lives can be deceptive and endanger — or at least slow — our progress.

We all too often wonder if we'll repeat the process. What stinks is if we don't analyze what happened and put it behind us, we're more likely to fail again. Success is what we strive for, yet we're prone to rush from failure to failure without loss of enthusiasm, sometimes believing this can't possibly happen again. Yet, it's more likely than not!

Stop what you're doing — take a much-needed break and reflect on where you've been (mistakes) and what you want to happen in your future. This is not the time to keep a stiff upper lip and keep moving without reviewing your past.

This statement could also apply to the mental and perhaps physical hell of finding ourselves in murky water, sinking faster by the minute.

The point: Let's review, keep moving with a set mission of reinventing ourselves with defined goals, and not become stagnant in our thinking or actions.

How does this apply to your life?

Sometimes we have to fight our way out of our stinking thinking or negative mindset. The attitude of "whatever it takes" is a good fallback strategy. When life seems too messy to keep going and your mind is befuddled and you can't think straight, then fall back, regroup, and try again.

You are alive today for a purpose! Believe that!

Forgiveness vs. Bitterness

You have a choice to forgive and move on or hold on to your grudges and personal failures and just squat, crawl or roll around in the shame, anger and disappointment until you're so bitter no one wants to come near you, not even yourself.

You can forget about attracting good into your life with these negative vibes. This is something you can't put a happy face on and move forward from. Like it or not, you give off energy — positive or negative — so it's up to you.

For example, sweetness may be drooling from every word you speak, but it won't hide underlying negativity. Change your attitude and watch the positive results.

Forgiving ourselves and others is easily said but takes effort. By now, we've listed our failures and most likely the wrongs we've done to others, perhaps when in the midst of our struggles or maybe not.

On the flip side, make a list of the wrongs done to you by others, whether intentional or not, for this is equally important in letting go of the past.

Find someone you trust with your secrets, preferably a counselor (which offers you some legal protection). Share your burdens, such as failures and times when you missed the mark and didn't live up to your own or society's expectations. From your list, without worrying about being shamed, share with your trusted companion, friend, and/or counselor.

Next, forgive yourself through God's loving grace, and forgive others. My cheat sheet: *No one can steal my happiness.* Then be prepared to make amends and say "I'm genuinely sorry" to those you've hurt whether intentionally or not.

However, this doesn't mean track them down to make them listen. They may not be ready for your candid apology and spit it right back into your face. What to do: Always be ready but not overanxious! Just believe the Universe will provide the opportunity for you to make your amends at the right time. Sometimes, our over-feeling or codependency can make us believe we are responsible for others' happiness when we aren't. If that's the case: Let it GO!

3

STEPS OF GRIEVING

By now we've realized that to move forward we need to take a step back and analyze to learn from our previous behavior. Get a pen and paper and start recording your life's story leading up to your present. There will be life events, people and places you'll never experience again in the same way. That leads us to the grieving process most adequately described below by the woman who made it her life's work for us to understand that process. These steps can be applied to grieve the death of our loved ones, as well as business and personal failures.

5 Steps of Grieving

Personal and professional failures require a grieving process much like that of bereavement. The five stages of grief according to the legendary Elisabeth Kübler-Ross are denial, anger, bargaining, depression and acceptance. However, we process these emotions according to our personal grieving process. Each individual has their own unique way for managing stress.

- *Denial* – Thinking this isn't or shouldn't be happening to me.
- *Anger* – How in the world could this happen to me?
- *Bargaining* – If you'll make this right, I'll do what you want.
- *Depression* – Nothing has worked, and it feels hopeless.
- *Acceptance* – It didn't turn out the way I wanted, but it's for the best.

When feeling stuck or depressed, reach out to a professional for guidance and/or medications to get you through the low spots. There's no shame in asking for help. There are people who can and will help. My personal experience is underscored by remembering to call on the name of the Lord. He will answer and guide you. I know because my face doesn't show I had a stroke now. That's the awesome work of God!

Practice Learning to Love Yourself

You are not your mistakes! If you're being shamed, blamed, or bullied, remember, you don't have to tolerate abuse!

Learning to love yourself may require time to forgive yourself and others to move forward.

You are here (in the Universe) for a reason, so don't quit now. Hopefully, you've learned from your failures and will be able to side-step stinking thinking in the future.

None of us is perfect, so at the very least, hopefully you'll be able to catch yourself and make adjustments.

Let go of the attitude that someone close to you should offer help in personal or business dealings. What it will do is upset you when they fall short of your expectations. I promise letting go of your troubles to the Universe and believing support will come when needed will take you further. I have been surprised over and over again by folks I didn't know but who apparently had my best interest at heart. These people came through for me when no one close to me was even aware of my challenges.

4

WHAT'S NEXT? - LIFE PLANNING

As a writer, I spend a lot of time in solitude, which is great for accomplishing my goals. However, human touch and conversation, according to research, are healthy and contribute to a balanced lifestyle.

I recognize times have changed. No longer do neighbors visit on front porches and catch up on the latest happenings in their worlds. The Internet distances us, if we allow it, from personal communication and friendships. That said, I've met people on the net I'd consider friends. Do we meet for coffee and chat? No! Could we? Perhaps, if in the same city and schedules allowed meetings.

So — what should we do?

- Make time to be present with family. Time flies, and it's easy to put off family gatherings. Celebrate the milestones of family members, including birthdays, graduations, weddings, anniversaries, and more. Plan a fun family meet-up at your favorite destination.
- Catch up with friends you've been meaning to see.
- Join clubs that are connected with your interests.
- Get involved with a church and/or social clubs to participate in their activities.
- Learn a new skill with people of like minds. Consider educational or social skills like ballroom dancing, yoga, etc.
- Find a hobby. For instance, reading, writing, a gardening club, tennis, golf, bowling, biking, fishing, watersports, etc. Get involved at regular scheduled social functions and/or other opportunities to participate.
- Make it a point to welcome your new neighbors. Invite them over for lunch, dinner, or a BBQ or potluck gathering. You'll find your general happiness level increases as you become more active in the community.

5

EXPLORE CAREER OPTIONS

Our careers are an important part of who we are and how we relate to the world. In chapter one, you made a list of things you liked and things you didn't like. This provided a snapshot of your personality and how that relates to your lifestyle choices of work and play.

For narrowing the possibilities and identifying your best career options, search the Internet for career testing sites. I typically lean towards Myers-Briggs (MBTI) based testing for its longitudinal value in connecting personality traits with careers along with the Strong Interest Inventory testing.

Once you've decided on your new career, begin your studies in the area of expertise you hope to develop. However, many times you can transition your existing expertise into your new chosen field. Other options include online, tech, or college courses related to your field. Please note a college degree is required in some careers like law and medicine.

Remember you don't have to do everything at once. Make a daily plan and do your best to accomplish your goals. If you fail, tomorrow is another day! Don't be hard on yourself as long as you're trying.

Fallback

Never lose hope! Life may look dark and dreary at the moment, but just as the sun sets in the evening, tomorrow it will rise again.

If you need help, call a family member, friend or counselor. When concerned that you might hurt yourself and have no one to confide in, call the suicide prevention/crisis hotline available 24/7. The number is 1-800-273-8255. It's free, confidential support.

Career Planning

Our work life is one of the most important components of our lives. The income pays our bills and allows us life's pleasures. To make something you're passionate about into a career would be an over-the-top experience. How do you do it?

- *1st step* – Define your interests and if unsure

glimpse back at the list you made from Chapter 1 of the things you like and don't.

- 2nd *step* – Align your personality with available careers

a) Seek out a career counselor

b) Take an online career assessment

1. MAPP – Assessment.com – I like this approach because testing provides the complete picture of your personality and career options. (Fee Required)
2. This is a free online site with some good information for ideal careers: *questcareer.com*
3. Google career testing in your city to see what's available. Career counselors and some colleges and universities also provide this service.

a) Read about the career that interests you. Would the day-to-day tasks interest and motivate you to do your best?

b) Talk to leaders in the field you're interested in. What advice can they give you about succeeding? For example, is a college diploma or higher education required, or does experience and/or tech school meet the requirements?

- 3rd *step* – Make a plan. Just as there are no two fingerprints alike, no two people are alike! Be the unique person you were born to be. Set goals; there is power in writing down your goals. Then check them off as you finish them and celebrate. Don't be afraid to expand your horizons. Getting out of your comfort zone is a must to create a better life.

- *4th step* – Don't believe everyone is on your side even when it appears that way.

a) Some of the best career ideas and businesses, either in startup or fully implemented, will have their naysayers.

b) Back to #1 – Know yourself and your capabilities. Is what you want to do feasible? Do you have the money to invest in education/and or business, and would you do so knowing the upsides and downsides?

Don't Go After the Latest Get-Rich Schemes

Don't search the Internet for the latest get-rich scheme or you'll lose lots of time and money. For example, the latest trend seems to be that everyone needs a blog. No, you don't unless it's relevant to your business and you're aware of the total costs. Blogging is more than just setting up a website. Key: Ask how the blog relates to your career goals. Let me provide some statistics (2) from Web Hosting Rating followed by 2018 predictions by a leading blogging guru:

- Over 2 million blog posts are published on the Internet every single day.
- About 6.7 million people publish posts on a blogging website regularly, with 12 million posting blogs to their social media.
- Ninety-nine percent of all the blogs started in a given year will fail. This percentage accounts for over a million new blogs.
- Note: Find your niche and research it completely before casting your business onto the World Wide Web.
- For anyone who wants to make money with a blog, link it to your existing business. If you don't have an existing business and still want to pursue the blogging life, I suggest learning the ins and outs and becoming a part of the cottage industry supporting the development and continued success of blogging. I'm convinced that's where the money is being made — helping those who have found blogging a good fit for them through careful evaluation.
- For the people who have taken the bait and started a blog, you need help from the best services. These are the criteria you need to look at before buying.
- *Number 1*: Choose the best hosting company to secure your blog.
- *Number 2*: Select products and services to promote within your experience and training. Note: The

closer you get to your interests and passions, the more it'll feel like play and not work.

- *Number 3:* Marketing — know how, when and where to market your products or services and the costs involved.

Breaking It Down

You don't need just a place to park your website; you need protection from hackers who'll fill your website with malware so that major search engines like Google, Yahoo and Bing won't list your site.

You need to understand website security methods and ways for finding potential customers. Also be aware that social media and digital marketing changes daily. Do some research and see how often you need to post to numerous major platforms with relevant information to capture a new audience and followers. (It's a 24/7 presence). This is not a relaxing place to be, especially when you think this is a dream job. Note: If you've already launched a blog, slow down and take baby steps. You don't need to be everywhere all at once.

How many times have you seen ads for creating blogs especially about travel, food or fashion? The ads say you need a blog to become financially free. Don't buy into this idea unless your business fits the above criteria. A blog needs to enhance your present business or be a tight personality fit for a new career. Blogs aren't required with some of the new apps/programs that allow you to post your offerings without a website. For example, today there are many new technical advances that streamline marketing products and services.

Get marketing right with the right offering, and the sky is the limit.

Learn something new every day!

The only way you're going to get better at your craft is to study what other "experts" are doing and make it yours by personalizing the advice to suit your personal and professional goals.

Everyone says you should find mentors — that's an easy catch-22 for the folks who see you spiraling into oblivion from a distance. You may ask where to find mentors without paying for them. You are right — you can't unless you're very lucky. However, remember the power of intention is also at work, and whatever is needed will arrive at the right moment when you believe.

I'd suggest learning the craft by studying books relevant to your ideas and learning from others, paid and/or unpaid. Then, put your best work "out there" and believe the Universe will support your efforts.

Other times, a mentor will show up when you're ready and it's your choice to embrace them or not.

I for one appreciate any handouts (or hand-ups), but I'm not going to lose sight of what got me there — myself through diligence and a God who loves me. The learning process is never complete, and having someone show you the ropes for the next step for success is a win-win! Perhaps, a divine appointment is on the way.

"Your desire to change must be greater than your desire to stay the same."
Unknown

6

HOW TO ACHIEVE YOUR GOALS!

There are two things that I've learned are important to success — time and resources to accomplish your goals. How often have you heard the phrase "time is money"? Well, it is! When you're spending time doing something, it's dollars spent. You could be earning money elsewhere or at least relaxing.

Solving the Problem

Have a clear objective of what you want to accomplish. This means stating (writing down) an objective that can be measured. More specifically, can you count it? Like dollars in your bank account? For example, more books sales — what does this require? Or selling more products. What do you need to do to accomplish this feat?

Let's look at the resources you need to accomplish your goals. Tools make a difference. I know you're probably thinking about hammers and nails. But there are tools to use regardless of your business industry. Whether it's a website for online marketing, social media, speaking engagements, or a retail store, there are tools and resource available to achieve these goals.

Depending on your objective, the tools may vary. However, the example foremost in my mind and experience is authors who already have published books. They need to continue promotions while writing new works. I didn't initially, and it cost me greatly. I have one happy personality to promote my work and another personality who is a much more focused, introverted person who writes mysteries and inspirational books. I'm learning to mesh the two for greater results. That's enough about me; what about you?

What Are You to Do?

Research the best promotional tools for your business. In my case, that would include book marketing companies to promote books, search engine advertising, Amazon advertising, or advertising via any of the major social media sites. The best advertising is word of mouth, which is difficult in our fast-paced economy. For authors and any business, positive reviews go a long way!

Make a calendar and schedule time for writing new content for advertisements and social engagement. Most social platforms advise against scheduling the same posts over and over again, or they'll penalize your site. So get creative and try new methods of delivery. Change major platforms and get more moxie in your advertising. Study what's working in your field and strategically implement your own version of marketing based on those findings.

Set realistic goals and time frames for completing the steps towards completing your marketing goals.

Implement new strategies. Yes, trust the new process, monitor promotions, and update as needed.

Today's business person has to be at the top of the playing field with presence and genuine offerings. Creating something of value for others will not only feel good but help achieve your long-term goals. I'd love to hear what works for you or not!

"Small changes eventually add up to huge results."
Unknown

7

YOU OWN THE POWER TO CREATE A NEW LIFE

CHANGE YOUR THOUGHTS AND WATCH YOUR LIFE change. You may ask, how is this done when negative thoughts stick in our minds longer than positive ones?

You're right! Studies show our worldview has a functional tendency to lean more toward the negative than the positive. To slip from positive to negative thinking is easy. The difficulty is reversing from negative to positive. However, it can be accomplished with effort and training.

Self-Talk

We create our existence, either good or bad, depending on our thought processes. Take a moment and monitor what you're telling yourself. Are you being defeated by what you're recording in your mind day in and day out?

When you find yourself headed down the wrong path, stop your thoughts and confront and dispute the negatives. Then replace the thought with a positive one. For example, thinking "I never get a break" could be confronted by saying, "The Universe supports me in all I do or say."

Judgments

A judgment is the ability to make considered decisions or come to sensible conclusions. We are taught from an early age to make judgments for leading and maintaining a healthy lifestyle. Knowing the difference between right and wrong, legal and illegal, is a positive mindset. For example, knowing that drugs are bad for us is a good thing. However, there are times when we turn negative judgments onto ourselves and others, including prejudices and indifference to people based on the color of their skin, how they dress, language and anything that differentiates them from us.

Making wrong judgments is a sneaky way for negativity to ooze into our lives and infect our positive beings. What if we stopped making judgments about others and focused on our own lives?

How to Stay in the Positive Mode

Gratitude: Studies have shown just writing out what we're grateful for can drastically boost our happiness and well-being.

Acts of Kindness

What if the next time someone was ugly or downright nasty to you, your response was to forgive them? I didn't say this would be easy! This is difficult for me. It hurts when you're dissed and you're trying your hardest to succeed. Sometimes, negative comments are the result of someone having a bad day and/or being envious of your perceived success, whether it's true or not.

Feeling victimized is a normal reaction. We all want to protect what's uniquely our own, especially our character and reputation. From experience, in the long run you'll benefit by losing the anger and letting the situation go without expressing your displeasure.

What about doing a small act of kindness for the person? Well, I just mentioned having zero tolerance for unkind and hateful, vindictive people. So now, I'm to turn around and be nice to them? Yet, my experience verifies kindness is the best choice and reduces the chance of a hatchet mob trolling you.

Doing a mind flip in attitude sends out positive vibes, plus being kind always puts you in a superior state of mind. Try being kind and see for yourself. It actually works!

For example, who doesn't love good food with excellent service? What if the waiter snapped at you, showed impatience, and gave all the nonverbal signs of not wanting to take your order?

You have choices. You can snap back, complain to the manager, go on social media and rat the waiter and restaurant out, and other forms of getting even. Does that make you feel vindicated? Probably not, for now you've allowed someone else's bad mood to spill over into your life. What a sticky mess.

On the other hand, you can smile at the waiter, place your order, or ask him to return in a few minutes after you've reviewed the menu. After dining and when the check arrives, practice a small act of kindness and leave a generous tip. Your kindness will flow over to others as the waiter is grateful and becomes mindful of their attitude towards others.

The opposite is also true. Express your negative feeling by leaving a penny tip, and the waiter's anger will hit fiery hot for the next diners. Ask yourself, do you want someone seething mad or depressed taking your order? I think not!

Here's another example from companies monitoring their brands on the internet. Customer service is a big deal on social media, and when a negative comment is made about a company, its products or services, someone will respond. Usually the first thing they say is: *We're sorry you're having a problem with our company. Please provide the details about your problem directly to us, and we'll make it right.* This response from the company quickly defuses a potential wildfire that could negatively affect their brand on the Internet.

Companies that are at the mercy of others through one-way review platforms don't have the luxury of responding. For example, authors have the potential to be hit the hardest from someone who just might be having a bad day. Although you may feel like saying something, especially if a review or comment was hurtful toward the author, don't go there. Leave it be and take the higher ground. Address your anger and disappointment through some of the steps you've learned earlier.

There are many signs along your pathway. You'll find the best of you when you take the high road free of hate, mischief and jealousy.
Inspired by Bob Marley

8

BECOMING HEALTH CONSCIOUS

THERE ARE TIMES SADNESS IS APPROPRIATE. NEVER think that you have to go through life with a false smile plastered across your face. You need to take the time, feel the pain, become aware of your thoughts and feelings, evaluate and correct them if need be, then let it go to the Universe — in my case, God as I understand him.

Note in this reference, I'm not talking about regressing to negative thinking and gloom-and-doom living. I'm talking about life situations or circumstances that are difficult — and sometimes out of your control — to turn around. For instance, a death of a loved one, the act of closing a business, a health crisis, the initial feeling of an empty nest when your children have reached adulthood and can live on their own (your initial parenting goal), divorce, job loss, and others.

For example, here's a very real possibility in today's world. Your website can be hacked, filled with malware, taken over by bots, and banned from major search engines. Even adding the most expensive roughriders to protect your business may not be enough protection. In the end, forced closures maybe the only answer.

Sometimes when everything is against you, just punt the ball.

Well, you evaluate what's important in life and be done with the rest! When a business tumbles like dominos, it makes you wonder where you went wrong. Could the Universe be saying, "Let's end this," or is some bad mojo working against it? Either way, it's a no-win situation deserving of sadness and grieving over.

So you may ask me, is this painful? The answer is yes! Can you move on? Yes!

Have you ever felt like you were up the creek without a paddle? Well, you've probably seen me there. I've seen my share of skip-to-my-lou-my-darling events and survived — a little beat up with blackened eyes but alive.

When becoming depressed, I've learned to put a limit on how long I'll be sad. Note to you — do the same and stop the spiraling. You know what I mean. You are more than your failures, and it doesn't matter who was involved.

There are times when a business skids into oblivion, forcing doors closed or dancing off the Internet right before your eyes. Rant if needed, then put the past behind you unless circumstances show differently. There are times you need to fight (legally) and others you have to suck it up and go on through a no-win situation. That doesn't belittle you — you've just learned another life lesson: Learn when to fight or not!

Glance back at the stages of bereavement in Chapter 3, and most likely you'll identify your initial personal response to tragedy. Remember when I said there was no correct response for dealing with loss? You could begin anywhere on the spectrum and maybe even revisit some.

I'll share mine for the record — anger, a normal response to things out of your control. My initial response is fight, and it's saved my life numerous times, even against warriors. There are situations when fighting smart is the bravest thing you can do, even if surviving means you're dead to the world. You'll be a winner and a wiser person in the end. Similar escapades have made great nutriment for my mystery novels.

As you confront the hurdles of life, you'll recognize your gut instinct of how you respond to let-downs and things you didn't see coming yet blazed right into your soft spots or your heart. If you need to run, then run and hide, for in the end you will come out victorious — or at least alive! Just know when to fight or take flight!

Be Aware Before Leapfrogging

Check yourself! Make sure you've gone through the renewal process described in earlier chapters before leapfrogging into something new. Just deal with it before it leads to depression.

On a positive note, a spark of adventure can open the doors to new opportunities. Trust that good things are in store for you.

Treat Yourself – Taking Care of You!

There are many activities we can pursue to enhance our well-being along with the mental, emotional and spiritual ones mentioned earlier.

Whether drawn to outdoor adventure or inside health regimens, taking care of you and your health is important. Living a defeated lifestyle often leads us to being overweight and out of shape along with melancholy or other unhealthy behaviors or addictions. You can get help for any addictive behavior connected to smoking, alcohol abuse, gaming, gambling, Internet, or others only you know about.

Step Up: There are gyms with non-judgment themes that embrace the obese and/or reluctant participants of healthy fitness schedules. Look them up in your city and make an appointment; your new life starts today.

Eating Right

Most of my life I've been blessed with being able to eat whatever I wanted. As I've aged, that's no longer true. I actually have to work at eating healthy. There are several ways of learning how to eat right. A nutritionist could provide some recommendations to suit your basic physical, emotional and medical conditions.

There are also some good nutrition books that'll help you get started and maintain your ideal weight. Educate your mind about healthy choices and follow through. Need help? Check with your local Weight Watchers group. You'll learn to prepare some delicious, healthy meals and make friends within the group.

Sweet Stuff

I love relaxing spa treatments and every feel-good moment they entail. Yet, recently I've been introduced to something new that I'm pleased to share: red light therapy. Note: I have no affiliation with these manufacturers.

My Experience with Red Light Therapy

I've been spending 20 minutes once a week at a salon offering red light therapy. I use the recommended eye goggles for protection and felt better afterwards. Please note this is not a tanning booth; you'll not get a tan.

What is Red Light Therapy?

Many users of red light therapy have benefited from this rather new technology for treating depression and skin ailments. It may be found in fitness centers and spas or from dermatologists and doctors specializing in bone and immune diseases.

Red light therapy is also known as photobiomodulation (PBM), low-level light therapy (LLLT), biostimulation, photonic stimulation or light box therapy.

Is It Safe?

Yes. Red light therapy is an FDA-approved therapy and considered safe. In fact, the original research for modern red light therapy came from NASA. Red light devices were used to limit bone and muscle loss in space. They also discovered that certain spectrums of red light allowed plant growth (for food) in space.

How Does Red Light Therapy Work?

These specific wavelengths of red light generate a biochemical effect in our cells that serves to increase mitochondrial function. This improves ATP (adenosine triphosphate) production in the body.

Why is this important? It activates the lymphatic system for potentially improved detoxification. It builds collagen and repairs sun damage and stimulates healing wounds. This is the short list for the potential benefits of this therapy. It's not a magic formula, and the benefits depend on the individual.

The importance of improved detoxification and repairs from sun damage were the deciding factors for me. After spending years enjoying outdoor sports and tanning, I was drawn to experimenting with this technology. However, please note this doesn't compare with the results from plastic surgery and dermatology.

"Don't make a change too complicated, just begin."

9

LEARNING TO LOVE AGAIN

Experiencing nature lifts our spirits. A simple walk outdoors daily will make a difference. Getaways or vacations to the mountains or seaside are bonus opportunities to breathe in the crisp mountain air or fresh salty air and expel the stress from our bodies.

Multiple research studies show our instincts are correct when it comes to relaxing. The hues of nature are therapeutic, especially the blue-green hues. Think about the ocean and elements associated with water — even rain, from the colors to the descriptive words we use in association to nature. Water holds cognitive, emotional and psychological benefits. Simply said, nature is medicine.

A walk on the beach, a stroll in the woods or park, or even escaping to your patio or balcony helps fix what's broken inside of us. It reduces stress, can make us more creative, and brings us together. Think about the last time you walked from the sandy beach into the gulf or ocean. There's something about those steps where you feel a connection to all of mankind. I can't explain the phenomenon – just try it for yourself.

Hurt from losses or betrayal leave gaping holes in our hearts that no man or woman can fill. Yet, don't despair and give up; there's hope for your healing, and you will learn to love again – starting with you!

10

SUMMING IT UP! THE NEW YOU!

Let's take a quick review of what we've learned that'll enable us to live our definition of a charmed, successful life:

- Journal daily
- Leave the past behind
- Learn something new every day
- Take care of your body
- Make a plan for success
- Evaluate your career options
- Be mindful; practice correct self-talk
- Practice small acts of kindness
- Discipline yourself to achieve your goals

Practice Steps

1. Write one sentence describing your new career/business.
2. Write down your immediate goals with a timeline for achieving results.
3. How will you evaluate and measure your results?
4. What are you doing to stay on track for improving your overall lifestyle?
5. What is your vision for the future? Example: Where will you live, play, and work? What does this look and feel like? What do you need to do to realize this dream? Write it down!
6. Take your vision and make it real for you. Pinterest provides secret boards where you can build your personal vision of your future. Play with it and post items that describe your new vision from a new career, home, cars, clothes, interior design and more.

If you have access to magazines, make a collage from clipping pictures best describing your new life and place it where you'll be reminded every day. Or purchase a picture from a gallery or thrift shop (super find) that's a reminder of the new you!

The New You!

You're now leading a healthier lifestyle, which includes eating nutritious meals, fitness, meditation, and learning new things while building the life you earlier defined as a success.

My wish for you: May peace flow like a never-ending river through your life and wash away the sadness from your past. My prayer is that your future life be filled with happiness, joy, good health and financial success as you seek your own truth. May all your dreams come to pass!

Peace and joy,
Carolyn Bowen

AFTERWORD

I hope you've received a spark of inspiration and motivation to become the best you. If you've enjoyed Cross-Stepping Your Way to Success, I hope you'll leave a book review at the source where you received the book, and/or blogs.

Authors depend on readers for recommendations to get word out about their books. I'd appreciate you taking the time to comment. Follow my blog for the latest writing news, contests and more.

If you want to learn more about personal and professional development, leave a comment. I'd love to hear from you about struggles and successes.

SPECIAL OFFER FOR READERS

carolyn@cmbowenauthor.com

REFERENCES & SUGGESTED READING

Dyer, Wayne. The Power of Intention: Learning to Co-create Your World Your Way. Carlsbad, California: Hay House, Inc., 2004. Print.

Groom, Winston. Forrest Gump. New York: Washington Square Press. 1986. Print.

Heiskanen V. Hypothyroidism: Could it be treated with light? Valtsus. Sept 2015.

Hofling DB, Chavantes MC, et al. Low-level laser in the treatment of patients with hypothyroidism induced by chronic autoimmune thyroiditis: a randomized, placebo-controlled clinical trial. Lasers in Surgery and Medicine. May 2013; 28(3): 743-53.

Kubler-Ross, Elisabeth, & David Kessler. On Grief and Grieving. New York: Scribner, 2005. Print.

Meyer, Joyce. Living a Life you Love. New York, NY: FaithWords, 2018. Print.

ABOUT THE AUTHOR

Carolyn Bowen was into life planning and career development before it was cool! With extensive advanced studies in psychology, adult learning, and career development, she has the background to guide you in becoming the best possible you! She's not only walked the walk but perhaps can save you a few steps in finding your niche — your purpose in life. She knows how to master cross-stepping as a surfer and life coach. She can guide you in avoiding wipe-outs while discovering your niche — your purpose in life. She's a well-read and beloved mystery author who calls on her life escapades and an adventurous, imaginative spirit to create entertaining novels. Her writing credits include "Cross-Ties," a historical romance, and "The Long Road Home," a contemporary crime fiction mystery.

Author pages in the Next Chapter Publishing
https://www.nextchapter.pub/authors/carolyn-bowen

Lightning Source UK Ltd.
Milton Keynes UK
UKHW041841030521
383075UK00001B/145